1.99

WHAT TO LOOK FOR at the
CASTLE

Philip Sauvain

Contents

Longman

CHOOSING A PLACE TO BUILD A CASTLE

Did you know that the first medieval castles in Britain were made of wood? Hundreds of years ago huge forests covered many parts of Britain; so there was plenty of building timber.

Building a castle

The king and the barons who built the castles usually chose a good place near a river or by the sea. Can you think why? Have you ever seen a castle near a river or by the sea?

People living in the castle wanted plenty of warning of an attack; so sentries were put on look-out duty. They could see a long way in every direction from the top of the castle. It was their job to watch out for enemy soldiers.

Motte and bailey castles

The best place to get such a good viewpoint was from the top of a hill. This is one reason why the first Norman castles in Britain were often built on artificial hills called mottes.

It was much more difficult for enemy soldiers to attack castles perched on top of a hill than those on level ground or in the bottom of a valley.

The bailey or ward

A spiked fence, called a palisade surrounded the castle. Other fences went down the slopes of the

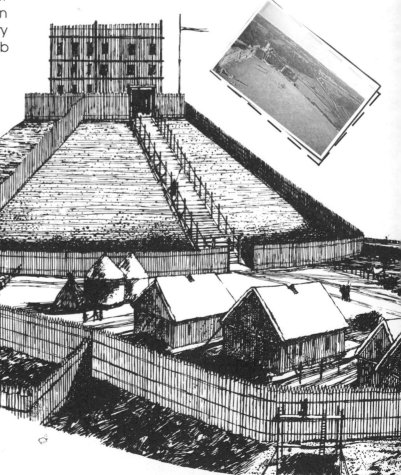

motte to enclose an area below, which was surrounded by a dry ditch or moat. The area within this fence was the bailey.

Almost all castles have a bailey or ward like this. It is usually difficult to see the original bailey since the wooden fence was later pulled down and a strong wall built in its place. There were stables inside the bailey for the horses, cattle and sheep pens and workshops. This was where armourers made, repaired and sharpened weapons, such as battleaxes and spiked clubs (called maces). It was where the bowyers made bows and where the fletchers made arrows.

The Norman Conquest

In 1066 William the Conqueror's Norman army defeated the Saxons at the battle of Hastings. Afterwards he granted land to his barons in return for promises of support at time of war. Many of these large estates were divided into manors and given to knights who promised their support to the baron.

They needed somewhere to live. Why do you think they built castles rather than houses to live in?

At first many motte and bailey castles were built across Britain to keep the Saxons in order. Wooden motte and bailey castles were cheap, quick and easy to erect. But they easily caught fire. So when things settled down the Normans started to build stone castles.

This is why there are no wooden motte and bailey castles to be seen today although you can sometimes see the grassy mounds where they once stood.

Visiting a castle today

When you visit a castle, climb to the top of the tallest tower and find out if you can see all the way round the castle. Can you see a long way?

Did you know?

that the Bayeux Tapestry shows us that motte and bailey castles were built in much the same way as you would dig a sandcastle on a beach! The tapestry was stitched by needlewomen shortly after the battle of Hastings in 1066. It shows workmen with picks, spades and shovels digging a ditch. They are piling soil and rubble into the centre to make a low hill or motte. A wooden palisade is shown on top of the motte.

Make a model of a motte and bailey castle

Use soft modelling clay like plasticine to make a model of a wooden motte and bailey castle. Put small sticks in the clay to show the castle and the spiked wooden fence which surrounded the castle and the bailey.

MAKING THE CASTLE STRONG

Imagine you are building a castle. Where do you think you would want to put the main rooms, so that they are safe from attack? Would you build a strong tower in the middle, surrounded by walls? Or would you put the living rooms in strong towers at intervals along the castle walls?

The keep

When the Normans built stone castles, like the Tower of London, they usually chose the first method of building a castle. They put all the main rooms inside a strong, tall, rectangular tower. This was called the donjon or keep.

The entrance was usually up a flight of steps in a building at the side of the keep, called the forebuilding. Since there was no way of getting in on the ground floor, it made it much harder for an enemy to attack the keep.

The keep could be defended even if an enemy got over the walls surrounding the castle. There was a well inside the keep to supply the defenders with all the water they needed. Many months' supply of grain (to make flour) was kept in a storeroom on the ground floor.

What other things did the people in the castle need? How were these supplied in the castles you have visited?

What was the chapel used for?

Do you know a castle with a stone keep in the middle, surrounded by strong walls?

The curtain wall

The wall surrounding the keep is called the curtain wall. This is because it shut off the castle from the outside world, just as a curtain shuts off people inside a house from those in the street outside.

Small towers, called turrets, were often built so that they jutted out at intervals along the wall. These made it easier for archers inside the castle to fire arrows at enemy soldiers who might otherwise approach close to the wall without being seen from the battlements above.

Round towers

Later castle builders thought of better ways of building a castle. Instead of rectangular towers they made them round. This was because a round wall is much stronger than one with square edges. You could chip off pieces of stone at the corner of a square building with a sledge hammer. It was much harder to do so on a round tower.

The later castle builders made the castle's defences even stronger by erecting massive towers at intervals along the wall. These towers had another purpose, since they could also be used to house many of the rooms needed by the people who lived in the castle. There was no need to build a separate keep in the middle.

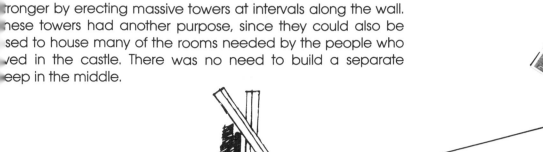

Did you know?

that castle builders in the reign of Edward I (about seven hundred years ago) had the clever idea of building two walls – one inside the other? the inner wall was higher than the outer wall? This was so that archers could fire over the heads of those defending the outer wall. Even if an enemy soldier got through the outer ring of defences he was trapped between the inner and outer walls. This type of castle was called a concentric castle – meaning one with an inner and outer circle of walls.

Make a model of a keep

It is easy to make a model of a keep because it is tall and square in shape.

Glue two or three empty packets together, such as those which hold cornflakes or washing powder. Open the flaps at the top and cut out battlements like those shown in the pictures in this book. Cover the outside of your model with brown paper and paint or cut out gateways and narrow windows (arrow slits).

HOW THE CASTLE WAS BUILT

Can you imagine what a medieval building site looked like, several hundred years ago, when a castle was being built? A good place to do this is at a point where a castle's walls are in ruins.

Stonemasons

The building site of a castle was crowded from dawn to dusk as stonemasons shaped blocks of stone taken from quarries.

These were often brought to the site of the castle by cart after a journey by barge along the coast or up a river.

Workmen dragged the stones to where they were needed on wooden sleds (a sledge on dry land) or wheeled them in simple wheelbarrows. It was heavy back-breaking work – especially when the blocks of stone had to be carried to the top of a tower or pulled up a long wooden ramp (like a slide at a children's playground).

Other workmen prepared the mortar (a type of cement). When it set hard it stuck a stone to the other stones in the wall.

Scaffolding

Since castle walls and towers are high the stonemasons needed wooden scaffolding so they could work in safety. This was very similar to the steel scaffolding you can see today.

Carpenters

Carpenters made doors for the rooms in the castle and shutters for the slits in the walls which acted as windows.

People did not use glass then for windows. But slits in the wall made the inside of the castle bitterly cold

in winter. Wooden shutters were used to keep in the heat from the huge fires which burned inside the great hall of the castle.

Castles cost a lot of money to build, although the sums which were paid to workmen seem tiny compared with wages and prices today. Huge amounts of building materials were needed.

Conway Castle in North Wales was built about seven hundred years ago. For one year's work alone, the workmen on the site of the castle needed 125,000 nails, 2,000 wooden poles for scaffolding and 25,000 wooden planks.

A picture strip

What jobs do you think the castle builders had to do first of all? What do you think the last jobs were? Was it like building a modern home? Draw a cartoon picture strip to show how a castle was built. Your pictures could be similar to those to be seen in books such as 'Asterix the Gaul'.

PROTECTING THE WALLS

The earliest motte and bailey castles were usually surrounded by a dry ditch or moat.

Moats

Dry moats made it difficult for an enemy to attack since soldiers could hardly fire their weapons as they climbed down into the moat. Iron spikes set in the ground made their task much harder. Later castles were surrounded by a moat filled with water from a stream which had been dammed up for that purpose.

Siege engines

The walls of the castle had to be protected against attack. The builders knew that enemy soldiers attacking a castle would use siege engines, called mangonels and trebuchets, to hurl large stones at the walls.

Mangonels

The mangonel was a clever machine, just like a giant catapult. It worked by twisting a cable or rope, so that when it was released it acted like a piece of elastic and flung a stone or javelin through the air.

Trebuchets

The trebuchet was bigger and worked like a giant see-saw. The stone to be fired was placed in a sling attached to one arm of the trebuchet. A much heavier weight was placed on the other arm. When this was dropped suddenly it caused the other end to jerk forward, causing the stone in the sling to be

hurled forward. In this way large stones could be fired to land inside the bailey of a castle.

Siege engines helped an attacking army to fire missiles at the castle walls and at the gates, hopefully breaking them down.

Thick walls

This is one reason why the castle builders made their walls so thick. Huge stones catapulted with great force could damage the battlements and break off stones at the corners of the walls. This was another good reason for building round towers.

The defenders in the castle knew there was always a danger that sappers would try to tunnel their way under the castle walls. This is one reason why the later castle builders sometimes surrounded the castle walls with a deep moat filled with water. Then if the sappers dug a tunnel, water from the moat would flood in, before they could light their fires!

Did you know?

that engineers, called sappers, could tunnel under the walls and cause them to collapse? They were called sappers because the holes and tunnels they made were called saps. The words engineer and sapper are still used in the modern army today.
As the sappers dug their tunnel, they used wooden logs to prop up the roof behind them. When they reached a position immediately below the castle wall they piled up kindling wood, set fire to it and then ran back down the tunnel to the safety of their camp.
If the fire caught hold it burned through the props and caused the tunnel roof to cave in. With luck this made the castle wall collapse. Enemy soldiers could then rush forward through the gap in the wall.
This worked well with square walls. It was more difficult with round towers.

A plan of attack

When you visit a castle try to imagine how you would have tried to capture it six or seven hundred years ago. Which parts of the castle would have been targets for your giant catapults? Where do you think your engineers could have tried to dig tunnels? Which parts of the castle would be easier to attack? How would you have crossed the moat? Use toy soldiers and a plan of the castle in the guidebook to draw up a plan of attack.

PROTECTING THE ARCHERS

Soldiers besieging a castle had to use wooden shelters called mantelets to protect themselves from enemy archers. Even these were at risk when flaming arrows were fired at them, so they often covered the mantelets with wet hides.

Arrow slits
The archers inside the castle, on the other hand, were well protected by its thick walls. Special arrow slits made it easy for them to take careful aim.

They knew it was extremely unlikely that any of the enemy archers could aim accurately enough to fire an arrow through such a tiny slit in the wall.

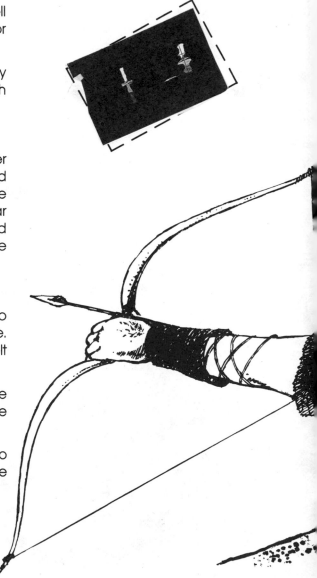

Battlements
It was more dangerous for the archers at the top of the tower or keep. They were more likely to be attacked by stones hurled by trebuchets. But, like the archers inside, they could also hide behind the walls. The top of a tower had gaps in it at regular intervals. These were the battlements. The gaps are called embrasures and the uprights in between, which protected the archer sheltering behind them, are called merlons.

Visiting a castle
When you visit a castle look out for the arrow slits and try to imagine what it was like to be an archer defending the castle. How far can you see from the arrow slits? Would you have felt safe there?

When you climb to the top of a tower or a wall examine the battlements. Do you think you would have been as safe there as the archers behind the arrow slits?

Later castles, built in about 1450, had holes to allow guns to be fired as well. If the castle you visit was built after that date see if you can find any gun holes like this.

You can sometimes tell that crossbows were used in the castles you visit if the arrow slits are shaped like a cross instead of a long narrow slit, which was all a longbowman needed.

Protection!

Which parts of your body do you think would be most seriously damaged by an arrow? How would you want to protect yourself against an archer? Find out from the pictures in this book what armour was worn by soldiers in the Middle Ages. How were the eyes protected? How were the legs and arms protected? What was the disadvantage of wearing a lot of heavy armour?

Did you know?

that the most effective of all the medieval archers were the men who fired the longbow? They had to be very fit, since the longbow was two metres in height and you had to be strong to bend it back to fire an arrow. A longbowman could fire an arrow with deadly accuracy over a distance of about 200 metres. Practised archers could have another arrow ready for firing in less than five seconds. This meant that an army of a thousand archers could fire 12,000 arrows at an enemy in under a minute!

The longbow was not in general use in England until about seven hundred years ago. Before that time archers used the shorter, less powerful bows – and the mechanical crossbow. The crossbow was in use in Britain about 150 years before the longbow. It had a shorter range and was much slower in use. Its main advantage was that almost anyone could use it, since a trigger was used to fire the bolt or quarrel (as it was called). You held it sideways when it was fired.

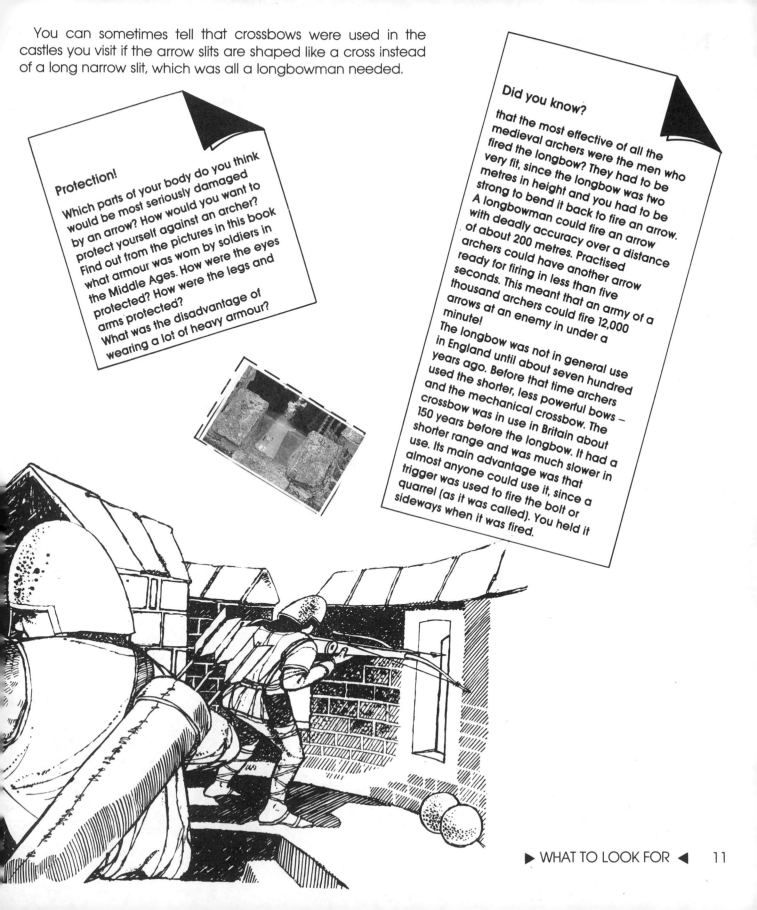

DEFENDING THE CASTLE ENTRANCE

Have you noticed that the entrance is usually the most strongly fortified part of a castle? Why did the castle builders think this was a weakpoint in the castle?

The drawbridge

Although the walls of a castle could be made very thick, there had to be a gap for a door or gateway to allow soldiers and carts through into the courtyard of the castle.

If the castle was surrounded by a moat there also had to be some way of crossing over the moat. A stone bridge was fine – but it was also a weak point if the castle was besieged.

The problem was solved when someone invented the drawbridge. The drawbridge could be pulled up on wires or chains at night or during the daytime, if an enemy approached.

The battering ram

A gate could be battered down with a battering ram. This was a strong tree trunk with an iron head, called the ram. A team of strong men rocked it backwards and forwards so that it thudded and thumped against the castle gate or some other weak point in the castle defences, making it shudder and eventually crack.

The men rocking the battering ram were protected from arrows by portable shelters made of wood and covered with thick hides.

The gatehouse

The battering ram was always a serious threat. So what could be done to strengthen the gatehouse? One way was to build huge towers on either side of the gate, which were always guarded. The guards made sure that strangers did not enter the castle. Arrow slits in the side walls of these towers meant that archers could fire at anyone attempting to force open the gates.

You can see these guard rooms on either side of a main castle gateway – often where the castle ticket office is situated.

Scaling the walls

Sometimes besieging archers would fire a volley of arrows at the battlements. As they did so their companions ran to the castle wall carrying light ladders and tried to scale (climb) the walls before they were spotted.

Visiting a castle today

Look at the castle and see if it has a gatehouse and a drawbridge. Some castles have more than one and some even have an outer gatehouse as well – called a barbican.

Did you know?

that special siege towers were built by besieging armies? They covered the sides with sheets of leather to protect the soldiers inside against enemy arrows.

From the top of a siege tower like this archers could fire at the defenders inside the castle.

If the castle was surrounded by a moat they tried to fill it in with mud, rubble and brushwood and then pushed the tower across at night. If they got close to the castle walls they let down a drawbridge from the top of the tower, so that it rested on top of the battlements. Then the soldiers inside tried to rush across before the defenders could stop them.

A working model of a drawbridge

Make a working model of a drawbridge.

Use an empty cornflakes packet for the gatehouse.
About halfway down, cut out three sides of a rectangle, so that a flap can be bent forward to make a drawbridge.
Make two holes in the wall on either side above the gateway.
Thread thin string or strong thread through these holes.
Attach the ends to the front of the drawbridge, so that it can be raised or lowered.

UNDER ATTACK!

What would you have done if a besieging army had tried to capture your castle?

The portcullis

The guards had to have some way of shutting the castle entrance as quickly as possible. This is why the portcullis was invented. This was a strong gate with iron spikes pointing downwards. It was normally wound up on wires or ropes, so that when it was raised only the spikes could be seen (like those shown in the colour stamp).

The portcullis moved up and down in special slits let into the sides of the walls on either side of the gateway. Look for these slits if you visit a castle. Even if there is no portcullis there may still be slits in the walls showing that there once was a portcullis.

If the enemy came in sight the portcullis could be slammed down in an instant. Since it fitted into slots in the walls it was very difficult to push over.

Machicolations

Behind the battlements, the defenders of the castle often had something nastier in store! They had a pile of stones ready in case any of the attacking soldiers walked under the machicolations or murder holes.

You can often see them in the stonework which juts out over the edge of the battlements – usually above the gatehouse.

The defenders used these machicolations to drop stones on any unfortunate soldier who was fool enough to come close to the castle entrance.

Cruelty

Although a picture of a castle siege looks exciting, it was really terrifying for the people behind the battlements – especially for any women, children and old men who were unable to fight. They knew that when food started to run short they would be turned out of the castle at night and left to the mercy of a cruel enemy.

Did you know?

that knights and soldiers in the Middle Ages were much more likely to be rough and cruel rather than gentle, courteous and full of chivalry? Sometimes they catapulted dead horses crawling with insects, and other diseased animals into the castle. They often hanged the defenders of the castle when they captured it. Richard the Lionheart, usually thought of as a chivalrous king, beheaded 2,600 Moslems when he captured the city of Acre in 1191.

Defending soldiers were as bad. They used catapults to hurl blazing pitch and tar at enemy soldiers attempting to swim across the moat, setting them on fire.

Make a model of a portcullis

Use strong cardboard to make a model of a portcullis.
Use scissors to cut out the spikes.
Glue several strips of cardboard on the back of these strips to hold them together.
Or you can use about ten old pencils or twigs to make a more realistic looking portcullis.

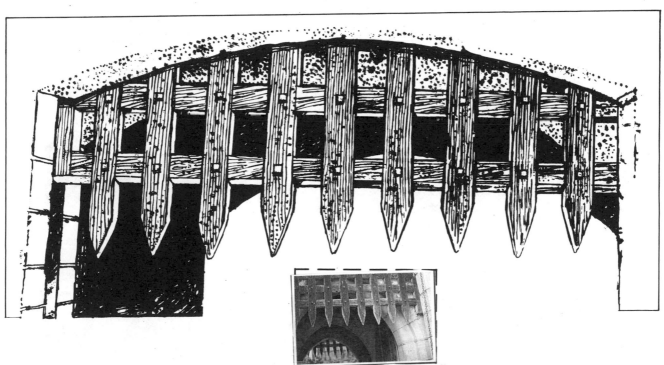

LIFE IN A CASTLE — EATING AND DRINKING

What do you think it was like to live in a castle seven hundred years ago? Can you imagine the castle in winter with snow on the ground or when it was pouring with rain? Do the rooms look comfortable?

The great hall

The main room in the castle was the great hall. In castles with a keep this was often on the first floor of the castle, reached after climbing the flight of steps in the forebuilding. In castles without a main keep, the great hall was sometimes made of timber and built so that its roof leaned against one of the walls in the courtyard of the castle.

Here meals were eaten and banquets sometimes held. Some of the soldiers slept on the floor of the great hall at night. Villagers sometimes came here to see the baron or to face trial if accused of a crime or failure to pay the baron's taxes.

The ruins of a great hall

You have to imagine most of this when you visit a castle today, since most are in ruins. The great hall may have large holes in the walls, or no floor like the one at Castle Rising in Norfolk.

Sometimes a fireplace is all that remains of the most important room in the castle – its main living room.

The kitchen

Castles with a rectangular keep rarely had separate kitchens. Meat was roasted on a spit in the great hall itself. In castles built at a later date it is sometimes possible to see where the oven was situated, although most castle kitchens are in ruins.

Cooking a meal in the castle

Imagine the scene at the time of a great banquet in the castle. In the great hall red-faced attendants turn a giant spit over the fire. Various birds, rabbits and hares are roasting over the hot ashes of the wood fire. Fat drips into a tray or flares up and crackles when it falls in the fire.

In the kitchen, cooks and their assistants kneed dough and pastry and put their loaves, pies and pasties in the oven. This is a cavity in the wall. A fire is lit in the oven and when it is hot inside, the ashes are raked to one side and the dough and pastry pushed inside to bake.

Water supply

Water for the kitchen came from the castle well. A well can often be found in the basement of the keep or the principal tower. If the people in the castle relied on a river, stream, or even a small lake instead, they might be in trouble at time of siege. If enemy soldiers could foul up the water supply they were sure to win, as no one can live long without fresh water.

When you visit a castle, see if you can find the castle well, the kitchens, the storehouses where corn was stored and the great hall. Are they close to one another?

Did you know?

that a meal in a castle could last many hours and that some medieval banquets were enormous? at one royal banquet the guests were served 90 pigs, 5,000 chickens and 10,000 eels – to say nothing of 70 swans and peacocks and over 1,000 rabbits, hares and partridges! At such a banquet guests also consumed thousands of loaves of bread and thousands of litres of ale and wine.

Painting a picture

After you have visited a medieval castle, paint a picture of a scene in the castle as it might have looked in the Middle Ages. You could show a siege or a great feast. Use pictures or modern photographs in the castle guide to help you show what it might have looked like several hundred years ago.

LIFE IN A CASTLE — WORK AND PLAY

Can you think what it must have been like to sleep in a castle in the Middle Ages? Do you think that castles are ghostly?

The solar

Although many of the people who lived in castles were soldiers, there were women and children as well. The baron's wife sometimes had a special sitting room, called a solar. It was here that she could do her needlework and look after her children.

Sometimes you can see a room in a castle with a big fireplace which looks as if it might once have been a warm and pleasant place in which to live.

Bedrooms

It is not easy to find rooms which were bedrooms. Most castles are in ruins today. Those in good condition have almost always been used for long periods of time and been altered since they were first built. So any bedrooms you see may be fairly new and nothing like as old as the castle gateway or its battlements.

Toilet facilities

Nowadays almost every home has its own bathroom with hot and cold running water and a lavatory.

Comforts like these were not to be found in a medieval castle. Only a few had a piped water supply. Instead they relied on water drawn from a castle well. However, they did have lavatories set inside the thick castle walls. These were called garderobes and sometimes they emptied out into the castle moat below.

The dungeons

The worst place in the castle was the dungeon. You can sometimes reach it by going down a spiral staircase. But there are castles where the dungeon is believed to have been a room with only one entrance – a hole in the roof! Why do you think it was built like this?

It does not require much imagination to picture what it was like to be thrown into the dungeons – to live there in the dark, wondering what your captors were going to do. In Carlisle Castle you can even see the carvings made by prisoners hundreds of years ago.

At work

Living in a castle was hard work for most of the inhabitants. Many were craftsmen employed to look after the castle buildings, such as the stonemasons and carpenters. Armourers made and repaired weapons and armour. Stable lads looked after the horses. The priest was in charge of the castle chapel and took prayers there every day.

At play

Much of the everyday life of the baron and other nobles in the castle was taken up with hunting. In this way they could improve their skills as horsemen and their ability to hunt down prey.

It was also a good way to kill fresh meat (venison from deer) as a change from mutton and salted beef.

Sometimes there were tournaments at which the men at arms in the castle could take part in mock fights and challenge other knights to a joust with a lance.

Did you know?

that spiral staircases were built in the towers, so that the spiral twisted to the right as you climbed the steps? This meant that a right-handed soldier with a sword in his hand could swing it freely from the top of the steps. How did this hamper a right-handed swordsman coming up the steps?

A picture story

Write an adventure story illustrated with pictures, based on what you have seen on a castle visit.
Make your story as exciting as possible. It might begin like this:
"The drawbridge started to rise as the last horseman galloped under the portcullis ..."
Or, act out a scene telling the story of a day in the life of a child in the castle.

CASTLE CROSSWORD

Across

1   . . . . . Hall to be found in a Norman Keep (5)
4   The Lord of the . . . . . had a . . . . . house (5)
6    (3)
7   French castle (7)
9   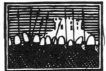 (6)
11 Another name for the bailey (4)
13 If you were hiding in the bushes it was not a good idea to do this when the enemy archers looked your way (4)
14 Vic and Tim get an arrow in the back (6)
17 This type of wall surrounded the castle (7)
18 What you did on benches at a meal in the castle (3)
19 (5)
20 Enemy soldiers with ladders tried to do this to the walls (5)

Down

1   The King made a . . . . . of land to the lords and knights who served him (5)
2   Female sheep (3)
3   You usually need this nowadays to gain entry to a castle (6)

You can find the answers on page 24.

4   (4)
5   This type of tower was harder to attack than one that was square (5)
8   Just the right amount (5)
10 Many castles were situated near one (5)
12 These huge bogeymen live in castles in fairy tales (6)
13  (5)   15  (5)
16 Go through this to enter the castle (4)
18 Many castles were situated near this as well as a 10 down (3)

WORD SEARCH

this WORD-SEARCH, twenty-one of the many interesting things you are likely to see on a visit a castle have been hidden. The easiest to find are those which read from LEFT to RIGHT the normal way – such as S P I R A L S T A I R C A S E. Other words read from RIGHT to LEFT; m TOP to BOTTOM; from BOTTOM to TOP; DIAGONALLY DOWN; DIAGONALLY UP. See if you can find all features. (Answers on page 24.)

```
S  P  I  R  A  L  S  T  A  I  R  C  A  S  E
N  D  R  A  W  B  R  I  D  G  E  G  I  T  T
B  U  E  S  U  O  H  E  T  A  G  A  T  K  L
A  N  W  C  G  F  D  U  N  G  E  O  N  S  U
E  B  O  R  E  D  R  A  G  W  M  M  R  S  M
R  R  T  R  L  S  O  L  A  K  E  A  P  A  P
C  U  R  T  A  I  N  W  A  L  L  P  C  E  K
U  T  B  T  C  L  R  L  B  O  A  H  C  E  I
T  I  M  A  W  L  L  G  S  Y  I  C  O  F  T
I  E  M  W  T  U  P  P  F  C  E  J  L  O  C
L  E  P  A  H  C  U  R  O  B  I  L  A  R  H
S  M  G  E  L  H  B  L  Y  L  T  S  I  C  E
W  R  W  C  L  L  A  H  T  A  E  R  G  A  N
O  T  M  T  S  T  N  E  M  E  L  T  T  A  B
R  H  E  R  I  E  W  O  I  S  T  U  R  R  O
R  I  E  O  L  L  A  W  A  R  K  R  R  S  K
A  E  N  P  T  T  L  E  O  G  R  R  S  A  E
L  S  U  K  E  S  I  L  G  N  E  E  C  L  E
G  E  O  N  D  S  I  L  L  U  C  T  R  O  P
```

gainden

► WHAT TO LOOK FOR ◄   21

CASTLE GAME

What you have to do:
(Ask a parent to help you if you get stuck.)
Attacking player – capture the castle by taking all the enemy's counters from the castle.
Defending player – stop the castle from being taken.

You need:
10 coloured counters for the defender and 12 counters in a different colour for the attacker.
1 Dice.

Rules
1   The defender puts 10 counters on guard inside the castle in the middle of the board.
2   The attacker then places 12 counters in the squares around the edge of the board.
3   Each player shakes the dice in turn. The attacker begins.
4   You can only move one counter at a time. It must be moved the exact number of squares shown on the dice. So if you throw a five you must move a counter across five squares.
5   You can move along a row from side to side and also diagonally. You can also change direction during a move – (eg. by moving two squares forward and then three squares diagonally). But you can't land in the moat; nor can you land on a square with a tree in it.
6   You can cross the moat in this way to get into the castle. But you must throw a big enough number to get across or to get back to the other side of the moat.
7   You capture an enemy piece by throwing the exact number on the dice which will allow you to put your counter on a square occupied by an enemy counter. BUT you can only move along a row or a diagonal to do so. You cannot change directions (as with an ordinary move).

Colouring-in
Why not colour-in the castle and the moat to make it easier to play the game?

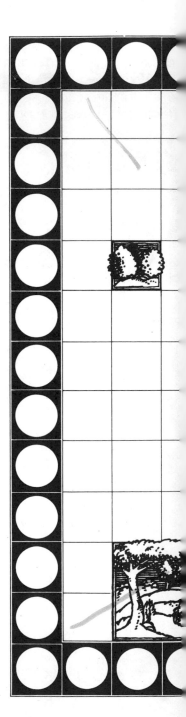

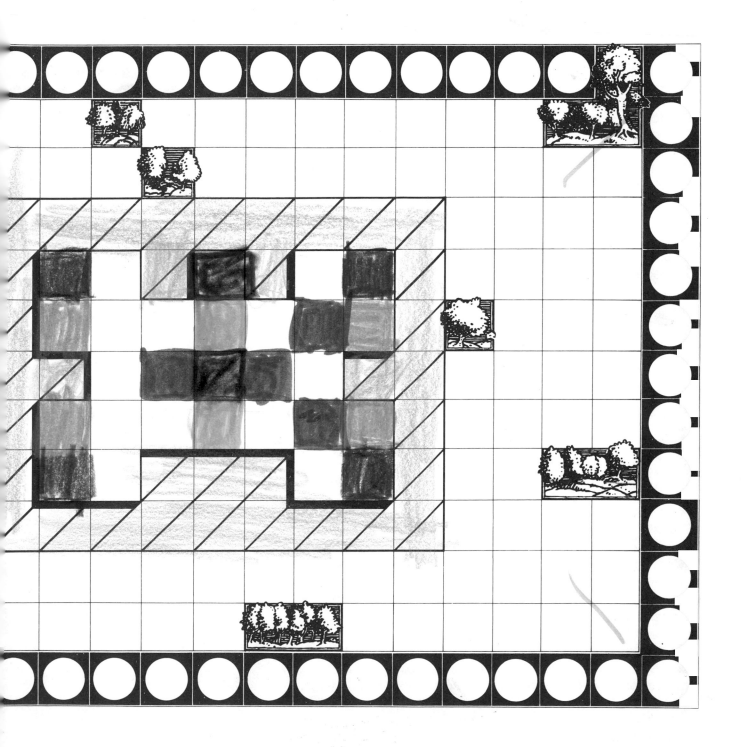

ANSWERS

Crossword

Across

1 Great
4 Manor
6 Axe
7 Chateau
9 Turret
11 Ward
13 Move
14 Victim
17 Curtain
18 Sat
19 Siege
20 Scale

Down

1 Grant
2 Ewe
3 Ticket
4 Moat
5 Round
8 Exact
10 River
12 Giants
13 Maces
15 Motte
16 Gate
18 Sea

Word Search

Drawbridge, Portcullis, Gatehouse, Machicolations, Curtain wall, Bailey, Tower, Spiral staircase, Kitchen, Moat, Well, Dungeons, Great hall, Solar, Garderobe, Chapel, Battlements, Turret, Arrow slit, Motte, Keep.

SOME CASTLES TO VISIT

ARUNDEL (West Sussex), BAMBURGH (Northumberland), BEAUMARIS (Gwynedd), BODIAM (East Sussex), CAERNARFON (Gwynedd), CAERPHILLY (Mid Glamorgan), CASTLE RISING (Norfolk), CHEPSTOW (Gwent), CLIFFORD'S TOWER (York), COLCHESTER (Essex), CONISBOROUGH (South Yorkshire), CONWY (Gwynedd), CORFE (Dorset), DOVER (Kent), EDINBURGH (Lothian), FLINT (Clwyd), FRAMLINGHAM (Suffolk), GOODRICH (Hereford and Worcester) HARLECH (Gwynedd), HEVER (Kent), KENILWORTH (Warwickshire), LAUNCESTON (Cornwall), LEWES (East Sussex), LUDLOW (Shropshire), MIDDLEHAM (North Yorkshire), NUNNEY (Somerset), NORWICH (Norfolk), ORFORD (Suffolk), PEVENSEY (East Sussex), RESTORMEL (Cornwall), RHUDDLAN (Clwyd), RICHMOND (North Yorkshire), ROCHESTER (Kent), ST. ANDREWS (Fife), STIRLING (Central), TINTAGEL (Cornwall), TOWER OF LONDON, WARKWORTH (Northumberland), WARWICK (Warwickshire), WINDSOR (Berkshire).